United States Government Accountability Office

Report to Congressional Committees

I0448571

September 2013

DEFENSE HEADQUARTERS

DOD Needs to Reassess Options for Permanent Location of U.S. Africa Command

GAO-13-646

GAO Highlights

Highlights of GAO-13-646, a report to congressional committees

DEFENSE HEADQUARTERS

DOD Needs to Reassess Options for Permanent Location of U.S. Africa Command

Why GAO Did This Study

A House Armed Services Committee report accompanying a bill for the National Defense Authorization Act for Fiscal Year 2013 mandated GAO to conduct an analysis of options for the permanent placement of AFRICOM headquarters. While GAO's work was ongoing, DOD announced its decision to keep AFRICOM's headquarters at its current location in Stuttgart, Germany. This report addresses the following questions: (1) What courses of action did DOD consider for the permanent placement of AFRICOM headquarters? and (2) To what extent was DOD's decision to keep AFRICOM headquarters in Stuttgart based on a well-documented analysis of the costs and benefits of the options available to DOD? To meet these objectives, GAO analyzed documents provided by and interviewed officials from the Office of the Secretary of Defense; the Joint Staff; and AFRICOM and other combatant commands.

What GAO Recommends

To meet operational needs at lower costs, GAO recommends that DOD conduct a more comprehensive and well-documented analysis of options for the permanent placement of the headquarters for AFRICOM, including documentation on whether the operational benefits of each option outweigh the costs. DOD partially concurred with GAO's recommendation, stating that the decision was based primarily on military judgment but that it will perform additional analysis of the location of the headquarters if the Secretary deems it necessary. GAO continues to believe such analysis is needed.

View GAO-13-646. For more information, contact John H. Pendleton at (202) 512-3489 or pendletonj@gao.gov.

What GAO Found

The Department of Defense (DOD) has considered several courses of action for the placement of the headquarters for U.S. Africa Command (AFRICOM) but decided in early 2013 to keep it in Germany. When AFRICOM was created in 2007, DOD temporarily located its headquarters in Stuttgart, Germany, with the intent of selecting a permanent location at a later date. DOD's initial goal was to locate the headquarters in Africa, but this was later abandoned in part because of significant projected costs and sensitivities on the part of African countries. Subsequently, in 2008, DOD conducted an analysis that found that several locations in Europe and the United States would be operationally feasible and less expensive than keeping the headquarters in Stuttgart. A final decision, however, was deferred until 2012, when the Cost Assessment and Program Evaluation office completed its analysis. Subsequent to this analysis, in January 2013, the Secretary of Defense decided to keep AFRICOM's headquarters in Stuttgart. In announcing the decision, the Secretary noted that keeping AFRICOM in Germany would cost more than moving it to the United States but the commander had judged it would be more operationally effective from its current location, given shared resources with the U.S. European Command.

GAO's review of DOD's decision to keep AFRICOM headquarters in Germany found that it was not supported by a comprehensive and well-documented analysis that balanced the operational and cost benefits of the options available to DOD. The 2012 study that accompanied the decision does not fully meet key principles for an economic analysis. For example, the study is not well-documented and does not fully explain the decisions that were made. Although details supporting DOD's cost estimates were not well-documented, the analysis indicated that moving the headquarters to the United States would accrue savings of $60 million to $70 million per year. The 2012 study also estimated that relocating the headquarters to the United States could create up to 4,300 additional jobs, with an annual impact on the local economy ranging from $350 million to $450 million, but it is not clear how this factored into DOD's decision. Beyond costs and economic benefits, the study lists several factors to be considered when determining where to place a headquarters. It ranks two of these factors—access to the area of responsibility and to service components—as critical. However, little support exists showing how the factors were weighted relative to each other. Moreover, the study describes how a small, forward-deployed headquarters element such as the ones employed by other U.S.-based combatant commands might mitigate operational concerns, but the study is silent about why this mitigation plan was not deemed a satisfactory option. In discussions with GAO, officials from the Central and Southern Commands stated that they had successfully overcome negative effects of having a headquarters in the United States by maintaining a forward presence in their theaters. In sum, neither the analysis nor the letter announcing the decision to retain AFRICOM headquarters in Stuttgart explains why these operational factors outweighed the cost savings and economic benefits associated with moving the headquarters to the United States. Until the costs and benefits of maintaining AFRICOM in Germany are specified and weighed against the costs and benefits of relocating the command, the department may be missing an opportunity to accomplish its missions successfully at a lower cost.

Contents

GAO U.S. GOVERNMENT ACCOUNTABILITY OFFICE

441 G St. N.W.
Washington, DC 20548

September 9, 2013

Congressional Committees

The President has established, and the Department of Defense (DOD) operates, geographic combatant commands to perform military missions around the world. Each geographic combatant command is assigned an area of responsibility in which to conduct its missions and activities. On February 6, 2007, the President announced that he had directed the Secretary of Defense to establish the newest geographic combatant command, U.S. Africa Command (AFRICOM), consolidating responsibility for DOD activities in Africa that had formerly been shared by the U.S. Central Command, the U.S. Pacific Command, and the U.S. European Command. AFRICOM began initial operations on October 1, 2007, at Kelley Barracks, Stuttgart, Germany, which was to be the command's temporary home until an appropriate and permanent location for the headquarters could be found on the African continent.[1] The department has invested at least $140 million to upgrade the facilities in Stuttgart, including major renovations of the office areas, family quarters, and an officers' club, as well as construction of a child care center and shopping facility. Moreover, AFRICOM has grown since its creation and, as we reported in May 2013, contributed to a nearly 50 percent increase in the overall number of personnel assigned to all geographic combatant commands since 2001.[2] An early planning document proposed assigning about 400 personnel, and DOD initially envisioned the command including large numbers of personnel from other civilian agencies, such as the State Department and the U.S. Agency for International Development. By fiscal year 2012, DOD had funding approved for 1,637 positions for the command, of which 805 were to be filled by military personnel and 832 by DOD civilians (see appendix I for the total numbers

---

[1]Beginning in 1951, Kelley Barracks was the headquarters location for the U.S. Army VII Corps, which provided defense to southern Germany. In 1992, when the VII Corps was inactivated and vacated this space, Kelley Barracks became the headquarters of the 6th Area Support Group (now known as U.S. Army Garrison, Stuttgart). Finally, when AFRICOM was stood up, it became the home of AFRICOM headquarters, and U.S. Army Garrison, Stuttgart, was relocated to Panzer Barracks, also in Stuttgart.

[2]GAO, *Defense Headquarters: DOD Needs to Periodically Review and Improve Visibility of Combatant Commands' Resources*, GAO-13-293 (Washington, D.C.: May 15, 2013).

GAO-13-646 Defense Headquarters

of authorized personnel for AFRICOM).[3] According to AFRICOM officials, approximately 3,900 dependents also accompany the AFRICOM staff in Germany.

The House Armed Services Committee directed the Secretary of Defense to conduct an alternative basing review for the placement of AFRICOM headquarters and to report the conclusions to the congressional defense committees by April 1, 2012.[4] DOD's Cost Assessment and Program Evaluation (CAPE) office led this study. CAPE did not meet the April 1 deadline, and DOD was granted an extension through July 1, 2012, to present its analysis to the congressional defense committees.[5] In January 2013, DOD issued the directed report. Our report is in response to a mandate in the House Armed Services Committee report accompanying a bill for the National Defense Authorization Act for Fiscal Year 2013 to conduct an analysis of options for the permanent placement of AFRICOM headquarters.[6] It addresses the following questions: (1) What courses of action did DOD consider for the permanent placement of the headquarters for AFRICOM? (2) To what extent was DOD's decision to keep AFRICOM headquarters in Stuttgart, Germany, based on a well-documented analysis of the costs and benefits of the options available to DOD?

To determine the courses of action DOD considered for the permanent placement of AFRICOM headquarters, we interviewed officials from the Office of the Under Secretary of Defense for Policy, the Office of the Deputy Assistant Secretary of Defense for African Affairs, the Joint Staff, the U.S. European Command, and AFRICOM. We also reviewed documents written at the time that AFRICOM was established and compared them with the latest statistics provided by AFRICOM to determine how the command's mission, size, and cost have changed

---

[3]About 250 of the personnel assigned to AFRICOM headquarters are located in the United Kingdom at an intelligence center that supports both AFRICOM and U.S. European Command. For the purpose of this report, authorized positions refer to military and civilian positions that have been approved by DOD components for funding for a specific year. These numbers do not include contract personnel.

[4]See H.R. Rep. No. 112-78, at 288 (2011).

[5]See H.R. Rep. No. 112-479 at 256 (2012).

[6]See id. Our work began in June 2012 in response to a committee mandate, but the CAPE report was not issued until January 2013.

GAO-13-646 Defense Headquarters

over time. We reviewed briefings and presentations prepared by various organizations throughout DOD since 2006. These organizations included CAPE's predecessor, the Office of Program Analysis and Evaluation, as well as the Office of the Under Secretary of Defense for Policy; Office of the Deputy Assistant Secretary of Defense for African Affairs; the U.S. European Command; and Transition Team Africa Command, a group that was established to assist in the standup of AFRICOM.

To determine the extent to which DOD's decision to keep AFRICOM headquarters in Stuttgart, Germany, was based on a well-documented analysis of the costs and benefits of the options available to DOD, we reviewed the CAPE study on this subject, discussed the study with CAPE officials, and requested and analyzed supporting documentation for the study's findings. We also obtained documentation from and interviewed officials with AFRICOM, the U.S. Central Command, the U.S. European Command, and the U.S. Southern Command. To obtain an understanding of how other combatant commands have conducted cost benefit analyses to inform decisions on headquarters locations, we reviewed the studies prepared by the U.S. Southern Command before DOD decided where to locate its headquarters and discussed these studies with a Southern Command official involved in preparing them. We reviewed criteria for conducting economic analyses from key principles that we derived from a variety of cost estimating, economic analysis, and budgeting guidance documents and compared it with DOD's efforts on the CAPE study. We also analyzed documents and interviewed officials from AFRICOM's component commands: U.S. Army, Africa, in Vicenza, Italy; U.S. Air Force, Africa, in Ramstein Air Base, Germany; U.S. Naval Forces, Africa, in Naples, Italy; U.S. Marine Forces, Africa, in Stuttgart, Germany; U.S. Special Operations Command, Africa, in Stuttgart, Germany; and Combined Joint Task Force-Horn of Africa, Djibouti, Africa. As discussed later, DOD did not provide us with sufficient documentation to enable us to assess the reliability of the data used to produce the cost figures in the CAPE report, but these estimates were in line with costs prepared by DOD in earlier studies.

We conducted this performance audit from June 2012 through September 2013 in accordance with generally accepted government auditing standards. Those standards require that we plan and perform the audit to obtain sufficient, appropriate evidence to provide a reasonable basis for our findings and conclusions based on our audit objectives. We believe that the evidence obtained provides a reasonable basis for our findings and conclusions based on our audit objectives.

Background

GAO has issued several reports on the establishment of AFRICOM and its components.[7] In 2008, we testified that DOD had made progress in transferring activities, staffing the command, and establishing an interim headquarters for AFRICOM but had not yet fully estimated the additional costs of establishing and operating the command. We also reported in 2008 that DOD had not reached an agreement with the Department of State (State) and potential host nations on the structure and location of the command's presence in Africa, and that such uncertainty hindered DOD's ability to estimate future funding requirements and raised questions about whether DOD's concept for developing enduring relationships on the continent could be achieved. In 2009 we reported that the total future cost of establishing AFRICOM would be significant but remained unclear because decisions on the locations of AFRICOM's permanent headquarters and its supporting offices in Africa had not been made. We also stated that it would be difficult to assess the merits of infrastructure investments in Germany for AFRICOM's interim headquarters without knowing how long AFRICOM would use these facilities or how they would be used after a permanent location was established. To determine the long-term fiscal investment for AFRICOM's infrastructure, we recommended that the Secretary of Defense, in consultation with the Secretary of State, as appropriate, conduct an assessment of possible locations for AFRICOM's permanent headquarters and any supporting offices in Africa that would be based on transparent criteria, methodology, and assumptions; include the full cost and time-frames to construct and support proposed locations; evaluate how each location would contribute to AFRICOM's mission consistent with the criteria of the study; and consider geopolitical and operational risks and barriers in implementing each alternative. We further recommended that DOD limit expenditures on temporary AFRICOM infrastructure until decisions were made on the long-term locations for the command. DOD partially agreed with the recommendations in our 2009

---

[7]GAO, *Force Structure: Preliminary Observations on the Progress and Challenges Associated with Establishing the U.S. Africa Command*, GAO-08-947T (Washington, DC: July 15, 2008); GAO, *Defense Management: Actions Needed to Address Stakeholder Concerns, Improve Interagency Collaboration, and Determine Full Costs Associated with the U.S. Africa Command*, GAO-09-181 (Washington, DC: Feb. 20, 2009); GAO, *Defense Management: DOD Needs to Determine the Future of Its Horn of Africa Task Force*, GAO-10-504 (Washington, DC: Apr. 15, 2010); GAO, *Defense Management: Improved Planning, Training, and Interagency Collaboration Could Strengthen DOD's Efforts in Africa*, GAO-10-794 (Washington, DC: July 28, 2010); and GAO, *Humanitarian and Development Assistance: Project Evaluations and Better Information Sharing Needed to Manage the Military's Efforts*, GAO-12-359 (Washington, DC: Feb. 8, 2012).

report, stating that in some cases, actions were already underway that would address the issues identified in our report.

DOD Considered Several Possibilities for the Permanent Placement of AFRICOM before Deciding to Retain the Command in Its Current Location

In 2007, the President directed the Secretary of Defense to establish a new geographic combatant command, consolidating the responsibility for DOD activities in Africa that had been shared by U.S. Central Command, U.S. Pacific Command, and U.S. European Command. AFRICOM was initially established as a subunified command within the European Command and was thus purposely staffed by European Command personnel. Because of this link to the European Command, DOD located AFRICOM's headquarters at Kelley Barracks in Stuttgart, Germany, where the European Command headquarters was located, with the intent that this location would be temporary until a permanent location was selected. In 2008, AFRICOM became fully operational as a separate, independent geographic command. Since that time DOD has considered several courses of action for the permanent placement of the headquarters. Initially DOD's goal was to locate AFRICOM headquarters in Africa, but that goal was later abandoned, in part because of what DOD described as significant projected costs and sensitivities on the part of African countries to having such a presence on the continent. Consequently, in 2008 DOD conducted an analysis of other locations in Europe and the United States, using cost and operational factors as criteria against which to evaluate the permanent placement of AFRICOM headquarters. Although this 2008 analysis contained no recommendation about where AFRICOM's headquarters should be permanently located, it concluded that several locations in Europe and the United States would be operationally feasible as well as less expensive than Stuttgart. Finally, in January 2013, the Secretary of Defense decided to keep AFRICOM's headquarters in Stuttgart, Germany. This decision was made following the completion of an analysis directed by the House Armed Services Committee in 2011 and reiterated in 2012 and conducted by CAPE. The study, which presented the costs and benefits of maintaining AFRICOM's headquarters in Stuttgart and of relocating it to the United States, stated that the AFRICOM commander had identified certain operational concerns as critical and that even though the operational risks could be mitigated, it was the AFRICOM commander's professional judgment that the command would be less effective in the United States. In announcing the decision to keep AFRICOM's headquarters in Stuttgart, the Secretary of Defense noted that the commander had judged that the headquarters would be more operationally effective from its current location, given shared resources with the U.S. European Command.

Original Plans for
AFRICOM Called for a
Headquarters on the
Continent of Africa

The initial plan for AFRICOM was to have a central headquarters located on the African continent that would be complemented by several regional offices that would serve as hubs throughout AFRICOM's area of responsibility (see figure 1). According to DOD officials, having a command presence in Africa would provide a better understanding of the regional environment and African needs; help build relationships with African partners, regional economic communities, and associated standby forces; and add a regional dimension to U.S. security assistance.[8] However, after conducting extensive travel throughout Africa to identify appropriate locations and meet with key officials in prospective nations, DOD concluded that it was not feasible to locate AFRICOM's headquarters in Africa, for several reasons. First, State officials who were involved in DOD's early planning teams for AFRICOM voiced concerns over the command's headquarters location and the means by which the AFRICOM commander and the Department of State would exercise their respective authorities. Specifically, DOD and State officials said that State was not comfortable with DOD's concept of regional offices because those offices would not be operating under the Ambassador's Chief of Mission authority.[9] Second, African nations expressed concerns about the United States exerting greater influence on the continent, as well as the potential increase in U.S. military troops in the region. Third, since many of the African countries that were being considered for headquarters and regional office locations did not have existing infrastructure or the resources to support them, DOD officials concluded that locating AFRICOM headquarters in Africa would require extensive investments and military construction in order to provide appropriate levels of force protection and quality of life for assigned personnel. Officials were also concerned that if the headquarters were located in Africa, assigned

---

[8]Africa has five regional economic communities, which are the Arab Magreb Union in the north, the Economic Community of West African States, the Economic Community of Central African States, the Inter-Governmental Authority on Development in the east, and the Southern African Development Community. The African Union, a continent-wide intergovernmental organization, established the African Standby Force, which has five regional brigades corresponding to each of the regional economic communities. The African Standby Force is intended to conduct peacekeeping operations.

[9]A Chief of Mission is the principal officer, usually the Ambassador, in charge of a U.S. diplomatic mission abroad and has full responsibility for the direction, coordination, and supervision of all U.S. government executive branch employees in that country, except for Voice of America correspondents on official assignment and employees under the command of a U.S. area military commander. *See* 22 U.S.C. § 3927(a)(1) and § 3902(3).

personnel would not be able to have dependents accompany them because of limited resources and quality-of-life issues.

Figure 1: DOD's Original Conception for Establishing Regional Offices in Africa

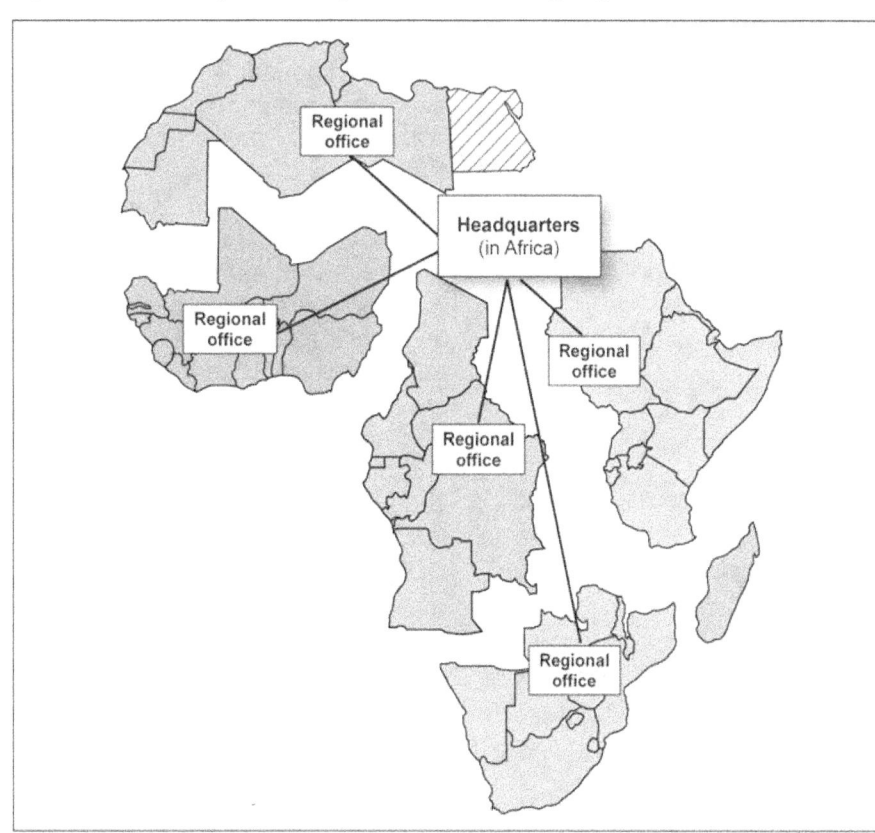

Source: GAO analysis of DOD data.

Subsequent DOD Analyses Considered Locations in Europe and the United States as Well as Merging Combatant Commands

In 2008, the Office of the Secretary of Defense's Office of Program Assessment and Evaluation conducted an analysis that considered other locations in Europe as well as in the United States for the permanent location of AFRICOM headquarters. It compared economic and operational factors associated with each of the locations and concluded that all of the locations considered were operationally feasible. It also concluded that relocating the headquarters to the United States would result in significant savings for DOD.[10] However, DOD officials decided to defer a decision on the permanent location for AFRICOM headquarters until 2012 in order to provide the combatant command with sufficient time to stabilize.

In 2011, the Office of the Under Secretary of Defense for Policy and the Joint Staff conducted a study that considered alternatives to the current geographic combatant command structure that could enable the department to realize a goal of $900 million in cost reductions between fiscal years 2014 and 2017. As part of DOD's overall effort to reduce recurring overhead costs associated with maintaining multiple combatant commands, the study considered merging AFRICOM with either U.S. European Command (also located in Stuttgart, Germany) or U.S. Southern Command (located in Miami, Florida). The study concluded that these two options were neither "strategically prudent" nor "fiscally advantageous," stating that combining combatant commands would likely result in a diluted effort on key mission sets, and that the costs incurred by creating a single merged headquarters would offset the available cost reductions. The study additionally found that altering the contemporaneous geographic combatant command structure would result in cost reductions well below the targeted $900 million. Subsequently, DOD determined that it would need to identify other ways to realize its goal of finding savings from combatant commands, and the department changed the timeframe to fiscal years 2014 through 2018. According to Joint Staff officials, DOD would seek to accomplish this goal by reducing funding in the President's budget request for fiscal year 2014 across all the geographic and functional combatant commands by approximately $881 million for fiscal years 2014 through 2018. To realize these savings, these officials stated that the department would reduce the number of civilian positions at the combatant commands and Joint Staff by approximately 400 through fiscal year 2018, but they provided few specifics. See figure 2 for a timeline of the courses of action DOD considered.

---

[10]The cost savings estimates from this study are classified, as is the list of cities considered as possible headquarters locations.

Figure 2: Timeline Showing the Courses of Action DOD Has Considered as Possible Locations for AFRICOM Headquarters

2007
- Locate headquarters and regional offices in Africa
- Temporary headquarters location in Stuttgart, Germany

2008
- Locate headquarters in Europe
- Locate headquarters in the United States

2011
- Merge U.S. Africa Command with U.S. European Command or U.S. Southern Command

2012
- Relocate headquarters in the United States
- Remain in current location

Source: GAO analysis.

In 2013 DOD Decided to Keep AFRICOM at Its Current Location

In January 2013, the Secretary of Defense decided to keep AFRICOM's headquarters in Stuttgart, Germany. This decision was made following the completion of an analysis directed by the House Armed Services Committee in 2011 and conducted by the CAPE office. The purpose of the CAPE study was to present the strategic and operational impacts, as well as the costs and benefits, associated with moving AFRICOM headquarters from its current location to the United States. DOD considered two options for the basing of AFRICOM headquarters: (1) maintain AFRICOM's current location in Stuttgart, Germany, or (2) relocate AFRICOM headquarters to the United States. However, the CAPE study also included a mitigation plan to address strategic and operational concerns identified by leadership as factors to consider in the event that AFRICOM were relocated to the United States. The main findings of the DOD study were as follows:

- The annual recurring cost of maintaining a U.S.-based headquarters would be $60 million to $70 million less than the cost of operating the headquarters in Stuttgart. The break-even point to recover one-time relocation costs to the United States would be reached between 2 and 6 years after relocation, depending on the costs to establish facilities in the United States.

- Relocating AFRICOM to the continental United States could create up to 4,300 additional jobs, with an annual impact on the local economy ranging from $350 million to $450 million.

- The study stated that the AFRICOM commander had identified access to the area of responsibility and to the service component commands as critical operational concerns. The study also presented an option showing how operational concerns could be mitigated by basing some personnel forward in the region. However, it stated that the commander had judged that the command would be less effective if the headquarters were placed in the United States.

In January 2013, Secretary of Defense Leon Panetta wrote to congressional leaders notifying them of his decision to retain AFRICOM in Stuttgart. In the letter, the Secretary cited the judgment of the AFRICOM commander about operational effectiveness as a rationale for retaining the command in its current location.

DOD's Decision to Keep AFRICOM Headquarters in Stuttgart Is Not Supported by an Analysis That Balances Operational Costs and Benefits for a Full Range of Options

DOD's decision to keep AFRICOM headquarters in Stuttgart was made following the issuance of CAPE's 2012 study, although the extent to which DOD officials considered the study when making the decision is unclear. The decision, however, was not supported by a well-documented economic analysis that balances the operational and cost benefits for the options open to DOD. Specifically, the CAPE study does not conform with key principles GAO has derived from a variety of cost estimating, economic analysis, and budgeting guidance documents, in that (1) it is not well-documented, and (2) it does not fully explain why the operational benefits of keeping the headquarters in Stuttgart outweigh the benefit of potentially saving millions of dollars per year and bringing thousands of jobs to the United States.

Analyses to Support Major Decisions Should Be Well-Documented and Fully Explain Rationale

According to key principles GAO has derived from cost estimating, economic analysis, and budgeting guidance, a high-quality and reliable cost estimate or economic analysis is, among other things, comprehensive and well-documented.[11] Additionally, DOD Instruction 7041.3, *Economic Analysis for Decisionmaking*, which CAPE officials acknowledged using to inform their analysis, states that an economic analysis is a systematic approach to the problem of choosing the best method of allocating scarce resources to achieve a given objective. The instruction further states that the results of the economic analysis, including all calculations and sources of data, must be documented down to the most basic inputs to provide an auditable and stand-alone document. The instruction also states that the costs and benefits associated with each alternative under consideration should be quantified whenever possible. When this is not possible, the analyst should still

---

[11]We reviewed numerous federal guidance documents related to cost estimating, accounting standards, economic analysis, and budgeting, and we identified key principles that we believe can be applied to CAPE's analysis of possible locations for AFRICOM headquarters. The guidance documents we reviewed include *GAO Cost Estimating and Assessment Guide,* GAO-09-3SP (Washington, D.C.: Mar. 2009); Office of Management and Budget Circular No. A-11, *Preparation, Submission, and Execution of the Budget* (Aug. 2011, superseded by an August 2012 issuance); Federal Accounting Standards 4 (June 2011); Department of Defense Instruction 7041.3, *Economic Analysis for Decisionmaking* (Nov. 7, 1995); and Department of Defense Financial Management Regulation 7000.14R, Volume 4, Chapter 22, Cost Finding (May 2010). We believe that these documents collectively contain broad themes that can be applied to evaluating cost analyses.

attempt to document significant qualitative costs and benefits and, at a minimum, discuss these costs and benefits in narrative format. CAPE officials agreed that DOD Instruction 7041.3 provides reasonable principles to apply in conducting a cost analysis, but officials stated that, as the independent analytic organization for the department, CAPE reserves the right to conduct analysis as it deems appropriate to inform specific decisions.

In April 2013, after the decision had been made to maintain AFRICOM headquarters in Stuttgart, Secretary of Defense Chuck Hagel called on DOD to challenge all past assumptions in order to seek cost savings and efficiencies in "a time of unprecedented shifts in the world order, new global challenges, and deep global fiscal uncertainty," to explore the full range of options for implementing U.S. national security strategy, and to "put everything on the table."[12] In particular, the Secretary stated that the size and shape of the military forces should constantly be reassessed. He stated that this reassessment should include determining the most appropriate balance between forward-stationed, rotationally deployed, and home-based forces.

CAPE's Analysis Was Not Well-Documented

CAPE's 2012 report describes strategic and operational factors that were considered when determining whether to place AFRICOM headquarters in the United States or keep it in its present location, and it includes estimates of annual recurring and one-time costs associated with each option. However, the analysis does not include enough narrative explanation to allow an independent third party to fully evaluate its methodology. Further, in our follow-up discussions, CAPE officials could not provide us with sufficient documentation for us to determine how they had developed their list of strategic and operational benefits or calculated cost savings and other economic benefits. CAPE officials told us that they did not have documentation to show how raw source data had been analyzed and compiled for the report.

The CAPE report, entitled "U.S. Africa Command Basing Alternatives," dated October 2012, consists of 28 pages of briefing slides. It includes a discussion of the study's assumptions and methodology, along with the

---

[12] Remarks by Secretary Hagel at the National Defense University, Ft. McNair, Washington, D.C., Apr. 3, 2013.

one-time and recurring costs of each option. The report presents a table summarizing the strategic and operational factors that were considered when determining whether to retain AFRICOM's headquarters in Stuttgart or move it to the United States. The table indicates that the most critical factors for a combatant command headquarters are for it to have access to its area of responsibility, partners, and organizations, as well as to have access to service components and forces. Working groups of DOD officials had compiled a list of factors considered important for a combatant command and had selected the factors they considered "critical." The list included access to the Pentagon, interagency partners, analytic intelligence capabilities, and European partners, including the North Atlantic Treaty Organization (NATO); ability to recruit and retain civilian personnel, embed personnel from other agencies, and leverage U.S.-based non-governmental organizations; and ability to operate independently without the need for agreement from a host country. However, the CAPE report contains limited explanation of how these factors were developed or why access to Africa and proximity to its service component commands were judged to be most critical. In follow-up discussions, CAPE officials told us that when they began their study they formed working groups to compile an authoritative list of strategic and operational factors critical to the operation of a combatant command headquarters, and that the groups independently developed similar factors, thereby verifying the comprehensiveness of the list and its relevance. However, CAPE officials provided no documentation of the meetings of these groups, the sources used to develop the factors, or the process used to arrive at a consensus in ranking the factors in terms of their criticality. According to CAPE officials, the reason they did not develop such documentation is that they viewed the study to be a straightforward analysis intended to be easily digestible for its policy-maker audience. CAPE officials told us that if they had anticipated an outside review of the study and its analysis, they would have documented the study differently. We therefore could not evaluate the methodology used in developing or ranking the operational and strategic factors presented in the CAPE study. Such an explanation is important, however, since operational and strategic factors were judged to outweigh cost savings and other economic benefits. Also, while proximity to Africa and to service component commands were ranked as the most important criteria for determining where to place the headquarters, some of the service components that were created to support the establishment of AFRICOM were originally located in Europe so that they would be close to the command headquarters.

For similar reasons, we were not able to determine the comprehensiveness, accuracy, or credibility of CAPE's cost estimates. The report itself does not provide sufficient explanation of how the costs were calculated or the effect of the various assumptions on the estimated costs for us to assess the estimates. Specifically, the report does not provide the sources of the cost estimates or the methodology used in calculating them. In follow-up discussions, CAPE officials explained that support for their calculations included e-mails and phone calls.

Finally, the study presented estimates of the economic benefits that could accrue to a local community if the command were relocated to the continental United States, but it is unclear how these estimates were factored into the Secretary of Defense's decision. In discussing the costs of the alternatives, the CAPE study presents a summary of one-time costs, including construction and the transfer of personnel and materiel. The study states that relocating AFRICOM to the continental United States may create up to 4,300 jobs (in addition to those of AFRICOM personnel), with a $350 million to $450 million a year impact on the local economy. However, the study does not explain how these possible savings were calculated, and CAPE officials could not explain how this analysis had been factored into the Secretary of Defense's decision.

Housing and Cost-of-Living Allowances Are the Main Drivers of Additional Costs Associated with Overseas Headquarters

CAPE's analysis estimated that the annual cost of providing AFRICOM personnel with overseas housing and cost-of-living pay was $81 million per year, as compared with the $19 million to $25 million these would cost if the personnel were located in the United States. These costs associated with stationing military and civilian personnel overseas comprise the bulk of the savings from CAPE's analysis. Although CAPE officials did not provide us with documentation for us to assess the accuracy and completeness of their cost estimates, they are comparable with those developed in OSD's 2008 analysis.[13] Moreover, our analysis confirmed that savings would be likely for both military and civilian personnel if the headquarters were located in the United States. For example, our analysis indicates that, conservatively, DOD could save from $5 million to $15 million per year overall on reduced housing allowances for military personnel, depending on where in the United

---

[13]The OSD 2008 analysis is classified; therefore, we cannot provide details.

States they were located.[14] In addition, an AFRICOM document states that the command spent more than $30 million in fiscal year 2011 on overseas housing benefits for civilian personnel, which they would not receive if they were stationed in the United States.

DOD's Decision Did Not Fully Explain Why Having a Forward Presence Could Not Mitigate the Disadvantages of Having a U.S. Headquarters

In its 2012 study, DOD tasked CAPE with analyzing two options—keeping AFRICOM's headquarters in Stuttgart or moving it to a generic location in one of the four U.S. time zones. CAPE analysts also considered establishing a forward operating headquarters so as to allay concerns about a diminished forward presence if AFRICOM headquarters were located in the United States. In CAPE's scenario, the forward headquarters would be staffed with about 25 personnel but would be rapidly expandable. It would also place an additional 20 personnel in existing component command headquarters. CAPE officials estimate that the annual recurring costs for the forward-deployed element would be $13 million, with a one-time cost of $8 million. CAPE added these estimates to its overall estimate of how much it would cost to move AFRICOM headquarters to the United States.

In CAPE's summary of its findings, however, there is no discussion of how this factored into the commander's conclusion when he stated his preference, or of how the CAPE study had factored into the Secretary of Defense's final decision. Operating with a U.S. headquarters with forward locations is the way in which the U.S. Central Command and U.S. Southern Command operate from their respective headquarters in Tampa, Florida, and Miami, Florida. The Central Command, for example, has a forward operating location in Qatar, and the Southern Command has forward locations in Honduras and El Salvador. AFRICOM already has a command element at a forward location—Combined Joint Task Force - Horn of Africa. According to Task Force officials, there are about 1,800 personnel temporarily assigned to this site at Camp Lemonnier, Djibouti. In 2012, the Navy submitted a master plan to Congress listing $1.4 billion in planned improvements to that site.

.

---

[14]We did not assess the eligibility of personnel for housing allowances. Instead, for comparison purposes only, our calculations assume that all members would be eligible for housing allowances at both European and continental U.S. locations.

When we asked AFRICOM staff about the specific operational benefits of having its headquarters located in Stuttgart, they cited the following: (1) it takes less time to travel to Africa from Stuttgart than it would from the United States; (2) it is easier to interact with partners in Africa from Stuttgart because they are in the same or similar time zones; and (3) it is easier to interact with AFRICOM's service components because they all are in Europe, and because the U.S. European Command headquarters is also in Stuttgart. An AFRICOM briefing, however, indicated that the strategic risk of relocating the headquarters to the United States would be "minimal," and also stated that establishing a forward headquarters could mitigate strategic and operational risks. CAPE officials also stated that maintaining AFRICOM's headquarters in Stuttgart makes it easier for AFRICOM to share resources at the service component level with the U.S. European Command, and that AFRICOM's sharing service components with the European Command makes it unique among the combatant commands. During our site visits, however, European Command officials told us that the two commands do not share personnel, even though two of the components are dual-hatted.

In its analysis, CAPE calculated the likely increase in hours that would be spent in traveling from the headquarters location to Africa if the headquarters were relocated to the United States. CAPE also estimated that if AFRICOM headquarters were relocated to the United States, the number of trips to Africa would likely remain the same. We believe that the number of trips to the United States would decrease. However, CAPE did not analyze travel patterns by individual AFRICOM staff. Our interview with AFRICOM officials and our review of travel patterns of AFRICOM staff indicate that being closer to Africa may offer few benefits for many personnel. For example, according to AFRICOM officials, 70 percent of AFRICOM staff travel infrequently. As a result, these staff could be relocated in the United States without negative effects. This is because the AFRICOM staff includes many support personnel—accountants, personnel specialists, information technology experts, and planners, among other staff—who do their jobs primarily at the headquarters. (Appendix 1 shows a detailed breakdown of AFRICOM staff by mission area.) In addition, our independent analysis found that about 60 percent of AFRICOM headquarters staff's travel in fiscal years 2010 and 2011 was to locations in the United States or within Europe. In fiscal year 2011, for example, AFRICOM spent $4.8 million on travel to the United States and $3.9 million on travel to other locations in Europe, while it spent about $5.2 million on travel to Africa (see figure 3). AFRICOM officials told us that travel to other parts of Europe includes trips to Berlin to obtain visas and passports, as well as to planning meetings with its components and other partners. If AFRICOM headquarters were to be relocated in the United States, the costs associated with travel to U.S. locations would likely be reduced. While some costs for official travel throughout Europe could increase, the travel that involves administrative tasks such as obtaining visas would be eliminated. In fiscal year 2011, this travel consumed almost one-third of all AFRICOM travel expenditures.

Figure 3: AFRICOM Travel Costs for Fiscal Year 2011

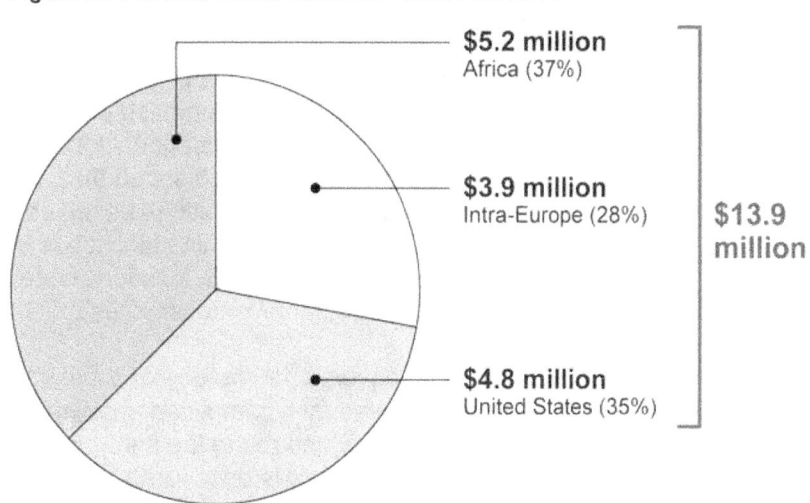

$5.2 million
Africa (37%)

$3.9 million
Intra-Europe (28%)

$4.8 million
United States (35%)

$13.9 million

Source: U.S. AFRICOM travel data.

Moreover, the view that AFRICOM could perform its mission from the United States is supportable, in part, because other combatant commands have operated successfully with a U.S.-based headquarters. During our review, we met with U.S Central Command and U.S. Southern Command officials to understand the extent to which their headquarters location in the United States affects them operationally. Officials expressed various opinions regarding the benefits of forward stationing personnel, and added that they are able to address time-zone and travel challenges. Central Command officials also explained that they manage partner relationships (including with NATO partners), overcome time-zone challenges, and travel to remote locations in their area of responsibility from their headquarters location in Tampa, Florida. They also stated that although they can quickly relocate personnel to a forward location in Qatar when needed, most of the headquarters staff does not need to be physically located in their area of responsibility in order to carry out their functions. A U.S. Southern Command official told us that they use video teleconferences with the components when they need to communicate with them. He also told us that the command has a forward presence in Honduras and in El Salvador.

Other DOD Studies Provide Examples of a More Transparent Approach for Comparing Cost and Operational Factors Associated with Basing Decisions

Neither the CAPE study nor the letter accompanying it when it was transmitted to Congress in January 2013 provides a complete explanation of why DOD decided that the operational benefits associated with remaining in Stuttgart outweigh the associated costs. Past studies conducted or commissioned by DOD, however, suggest that a more thorough approach to analyzing costs and benefits is possible. For example, unlike the 2012 analysis, DOD's 2008 analysis of potential AFRICOM locations ranked each location according to how it fared against cost and operational factors. While the analysis made no recommendation and stated that Germany was superior to all of the considered U.S. locations based on factors other than cost, it concluded that any of the examined locations would be an operationally feasible choice, and that U.S. locations were routinely and significantly cheaper to maintain than overseas bases.

Moreover, a 1994 study was initiated by the U.S. Southern Command and validated by a committee appointed by the Deputy Secretary of Defense to review and refine the analysis. The committee included the Assistant Secretary of Defense for Strategy and Requirements, the Principal Deputy Comptroller, and the Director for Strategic Plans and Policy, Joint Staff. The Committee's final report quantified and prioritized operational benefits to determine where in the United States to place the U.S. Southern Command headquarters when it was required to move from Panama. Although this study did not consider overseas locations and assumed that remaining in Panama was not an option, it nevertheless stands as an example of a more transparent approach to weighing costs and operational concerns. This study examined 126 sites in the United States and then narrowed the possibilities based on criteria that addressed the mission and quality of life for assigned personnel. The names of the locations under consideration were "masked" to ensure that the criteria were applied objectively. As a result, six locations were chosen as most desirable: Tampa, Atlanta, New Orleans, Miami, Puerto Rico, and Washington, D.C. Visits were made to each of the locations and the final tallying of scores, including consideration of costs, showed that Miami was the preferred choice. The committee expanded the analysis through additional evaluation of Southern Command's mission requirements and quality of life issues. Once its analysis was complete, the committee briefed the Deputy Secretary of Defense on its findings and conclusions based on three criteria: mission effectiveness, quality of life, and cost. In summary, the committee stated that if mission effectiveness was the most important of the three criteria, then Miami was clearly the superior location. If quality of life was the most important, then Washington was the leading candidate. If cost was the most important consideration, then New Orleans was the leading candidate. The committee's recommendation was for the Secretary of Defense and the Deputy Secretary of Defense to select the final Southern Command relocation site from among those three candidate cities.

Finally, a 2013 RAND study conducted in response to a congressional requirement for DOD to commission an independent assessment of the overseas basing presence of U.S. forces provides several examples of principles that can be used to determine where to geographically place personnel so that they can most effectively be employed.[15] For example, the study states that, because basing personnel in overseas locations is generally more expensive than basing them in the United States, DOD could consider configuring its forward-based forces overseas so that they can provide the initial response to a conflict, while placing in the United States the forces that will provide follow-up support. To inform the assessment of overseas forces, RAND examined how overseas posture translates to benefits, the risks that it poses, the cost of maintaining it, and how these costs would likely change if the U.S. overseas presence were to be modified in different ways—for example, by changing from a permanent to a rotational presence.

Conclusions

DOD's letter describing the January 2013 decision to maintain the command in Stuttgart was based on operational benefits that are not clearly laid out, and it is unclear how cost savings and economic benefits were considered in the decision. DOD's analysis stated that significant savings and economic benefits would result if the command were relocated to the United States, and our independent analyses confirmed that significant savings are possible. Moreover, the decision does not explain why using a small contingent of personnel stationed forward would not mitigate operational concerns. Our analysis of travel patterns and staff composition raises questions about why the AFRICOM staff

---

[15]RAND Corporation, *Overseas Basing of U.S. Military Forces: An Assessment of Relative Costs and Strategic Benefits* (Santa Monica: CA 90407), 2013. The requirement for DOD to commission the assessment appeared in the National Defense Authorization Act for Fiscal Year 2012. *See* Pub. L. No. 112-81, § 347 (2011).

needs to be located overseas, because not all staff would benefit from being closer to Africa—especially when other combatant commands operate with their headquarters in the United States. Key principles that GAO has derived for economic analysis and cost estimating, as well as a DOD instruction containing principles for certain types of economic analysis, suggest that the department's rationale should be detailed and the study underpinning it should be comprehensive and well-documented. Since making the decision to keep AFRICOM's headquarters in Stuttgart, the Department of Defense has sought to fundamentally rethink how the department does business in an era of increasingly constrained fiscal resources. Until the costs and benefits of maintaining AFRICOM in Germany are specified and weighed against the costs and economic benefits of moving the command, the department may be missing an opportunity to accomplish its missions successfully at a significantly lower cost.

Recommendation for Executive Action

To enable the department to meet its Africa-related missions at the least cost, GAO recommends that the Secretary of Defense conduct a more comprehensive and well-documented analysis of options for the permanent placement of the headquarters for AFRICOM, including documentation as to whether the operational benefits of each option outweigh the costs. These options should include placing some AFRICOM headquarters personnel in forward locations, while moving others to the United States. In conducting this assessment, the Secretary should follow key principles GAO has derived for such studies, as well as principles found in DOD Instruction 7041.3, to help ensure that the results are comprehensive, well-documented, accurate, and credible. Should DOD determine that maintaining a location in Stuttgart is the best course of action, the Secretary of Defense should provide a detailed description of why the operational or other benefits outweigh the costs and benefits of relocating the command.

Agency Comments and Our Evaluation

In written comments on a draft of this report, DOD stated that the 2012 CAPE study met the requirements of the House Armed Services Committee report accompanying the National Defense Authorization Act for Fiscal Year 2012. DOD stated that the CAPE study was not intended to be a comprehensive analysis to determine the optimal location for AFRICOM's headquarters. Rather, DOD believed that the study provided sufficient detail to support the specific questions posed in the National Defense Authorization Act. While the CAPE office did present the estimated costs of relocating AFRICOM's headquarters, the National

Defense Authorization Act directing DOD to conduct this study specifically urged DOD to conduct this basing review "in an open and transparent manner consistent with the processes established for such a major review." As we state in the body of our report, the CAPE study did not provide sufficient detail to support its methodology and cost estimates for a third party to validate the study's findings. Moreover, DOD's own guidance on conducting an economic analysis states that such an analysis should be transparent and serve as a stand-alone document.

DOD also stated that Secretary Panetta's decision not to relocate the AFRICOM headquarters to the United States was based largely on the combatant commanders' military judgment, which is not easily quantifiable. We recognize that military judgment is not easily quantifiable. However, we continue to believe that an accurate and reliable analysis should provide a more complete explanation of how operational benefits and costs were weighed, especially in light of the potential cost savings that DOD is deciding to forego.

DOD partially concurred with our recommendation. DOD stated that to meet the requirements of the Budget Control Act, the Department of Defense will consider a wide range of options. If any of these options require additional analysis of the location of AFRICOM headquarters, DOD said that it will conduct a comprehensive and well-documented analysis. We continue to believe that such an analysis is needed. Because of the current tight fiscal climate and the Secretary of Defense's continual urging that DOD identify additional opportunities for achieving efficiencies and cost savings, DOD should reassess the option of relocating AFRICOM's headquarters to the United States.

The department's written comments are reprinted in appendix II.

We are sending copies of this report to the Secretary of Defense and the Secretary of State. The report will also be available at no charge on the GAO Web site at http://www.gao.gov.

If you or your staff have questions about this report, please contact me at (202) 512-3489 or at pendletonj@gao.gov. Contact points for our Offices of Congressional Relations and Public Affairs may be found on the last page of this report. GAO staff who made key contributions to this report are listed in appendix III.

John H. Pendleton
Director, Defense Capabilities and Management

List of Committees

The Honorable Carl Levin
Chairman
The Honorable James M. Inhofe
Ranking Member
Committee on Armed Services
United States Senate

The Honorable Dick Durbin
Chairman
The Honorable Thad Cochran
Subcommittee on Defense
Committee on Appropriations
United States Senate

The Honorable Howard P. "Buck" McKeon
Chairman
The Honorable Adam Smith
Ranking Member
Committee on Armed Services
House of Representatives

The Honorable C. W. Bill Young
Chairman
The Honorable Pete Visclosky
Ranking Member
Subcommittee on Defense
Committee on Appropriations
House of Representatives

U.S. AFRICA COMMAND (AFRICOM)

Fiscal Year 2012 Authorized Military and Civilian Positions by Directorate, Subordinate Unified Command, and Other Activities			
U.S. Africa Command Headquarters Directorates	Military	Civilian	Total
J00 Command Staff	65	74	139
J1/J8 Resources	36	82	118
J3 Operations	105	94	199
J4 Logistics	43	37	80
J5 Strategy, Plans, and Programs	83	85	168
J6 Command, Control, Communications, and Computer Systems	22	52	74
J7 Joint Training and Exercises	12	9	21
J9 Outreach	12	19	31
Headquarters Directorates Total	**378**	**452**	**830**
Subordinate Unified Commands and Other Activities			
Special Operations Command Africa	133	47	180
J2 Intelligence and Knowledge Development - Stuttgart	81	119	200
J2 Intelligence and Knowledge Development - Molesworth	120	133	253
Security Cooperation Organizations	93	81	174
Subordinate Unified Command and Other Activities Total	**427**	**380**	**807**
U.S. Africa Command Grand Total	**805**	**832**	**1,637**

Source: GAO analysis of DOD data.

Note: Authorized military and civilian positions represent positions identified by DOD as approved, funded manpower requirements at the geographic command. Numbers in this table do not include numbers of foreign nationals employed by AFRICOM.

Appendix II: Comments from the Department of Defense

OFFICE OF THE SECRETARY OF DEFENSE
1800 DEFENSE PENTAGON
WASHINGTON, D.C. 20301-1800

COST ASSESSMENT AND
PROGRAM EVALUATION

AUG 27 2013

Mr. John H. Pendleton
Director, Defense Capabilities and Management
U.S. Government Accountability Office
441 G Street, NW
Washington, DC 20548

Dear Mr. Pendleton:

This is the Department of Defense (DoD) response to the GAO Draft Report, GAO-13-646, 'DEFENSE HEADQUARTERS: DOD Needs to Reassess Options for Permanent Location of U.S. Africa Command,' dated July 25, 2013 (GAO Code 351748). Detailed comments are enclosed with this letter.

The 2012 CAPE study met the requirements of House Armed Services Committee report accompanying the National Defense Authorization Act for Fiscal Year 2012 (NDAA), which directed an alternative basing review for U.S. Africa Command (AFRICOM). This study focused on several elements of the AFRICOM question and is not intended to be a comprehensive analysis to determine the optimal location for the AFRICOM headquarters. Instead, the study provided sufficient detail to support the specific question posed in the NDAA. Secretary Panetta's decision not to relocate the AFRICOM headquarters to the United States was based largely on the Combatant Commanders' military judgment which is not easily quantifiable. If Secretary Hagel sees the need to readdress the location of AFRICOM, the Department will conduct appropriate analysis, consistent with sound analytic practice, to inform such a decision.

Sincerely,

Robert P. Lennox
LTG, USA
Principal Deputy Director

Enclosure:
As stated

GAO DRAFT REPORT DATED JULY 25, 2013
GAO-13-646 (GAO CODE 351748)

"DEFENSE HEADQUARTERS: DOD NEEDS TO REASSESS OPTIONS FOR
PERMANENT LOCATION OF U.S. AFRICA COMMAND"

DEPARTMENT OF DEFENSE COMMENTS
TO THE GAO RECOMMENDATIONS

RECOMMENDATION: GAO recommends the Secretary of Defense conduct a more
comprehensive and well-documented analysis of options for the permanent placement of the
headquarters for AFRICOM, including documentation as to whether the operational benefits of
each option outweigh the costs. These options should include placing some AFRICOM
headquarters personnel in forward locations, while moving others to the United States. In
conducting this assessment, the Secretary should follow key principles GAO has derived for such
studies, as well as principles found in DOD Instruction 7041.3, to help ensure the results are
comprehensive, well-documented, accurate, and credible. Should DoD determine that
maintaining a location in Stuttgart is the best course of action, the Secretary of Defense should
provide a detailed description of why the operational or other benefits outweigh the cost and
benefits of relocating the command. (See page 20/GAO Draft Report)

DoD RESPONSE: Partially Concur.

To meet the requirements of the Budget Control Act the Department of Defense will consider a
wide range of options. If any of those options require additional analysis of the location of
AFRICOM headquarters the Department will conduct a comprehensive and well-documented
analysis.

Tab A

Appendix III: GAO Contact and Staff Acknowledgments

GAO Contact

John Pendleton, Director, (202) 512-3489

Staff Acknowledgments

In addition to the contact named above, Guy LoFaro, Assistant Director; Nicole Harris; Charles Perdue; Carol Petersen; Beverly Schladt; Mike Shaughnessy; Amie Steele; Grant Sutton; and Cheryl Weissman made major contributions to this report.

GAO's Mission	The Government Accountability Office, the audit, evaluation, and investigative arm of Congress, exists to support Congress in meeting its constitutional responsibilities and to help improve the performance and accountability of the federal government for the American people. GAO examines the use of public funds; evaluates federal programs and policies; and provides analyses, recommendations, and other assistance to help Congress make informed oversight, policy, and funding decisions. GAO's commitment to good government is reflected in its core values of accountability, integrity, and reliability.
Obtaining Copies of GAO Reports and Testimony	The fastest and easiest way to obtain copies of GAO documents at no cost is through GAO's website (http://www.gao.gov). Each weekday afternoon, GAO posts on its website newly released reports, testimony, and correspondence. To have GAO e-mail you a list of newly posted products, go to http://www.gao.gov and select "E-mail Updates."
Order by Phone	The price of each GAO publication reflects GAO's actual cost of production and distribution and depends on the number of pages in the publication and whether the publication is printed in color or black and white. Pricing and ordering information is posted on GAO's website, http://www.gao.gov/ordering.htm. Place orders by calling (202) 512-6000, toll free (866) 801-7077, or TDD (202) 512-2537. Orders may be paid for using American Express, Discover Card, MasterCard, Visa, check, or money order. Call for additional information.
Connect with GAO	Connect with GAO on Facebook, Flickr, Twitter, and YouTube. Subscribe to our RSS Feeds or E-mail Updates. Listen to our Podcasts. Visit GAO on the web at www.gao.gov.
To Report Fraud, Waste, and Abuse in Federal Programs	Contact: Website: http://www.gao.gov/fraudnet/fraudnet.htm E-mail: fraudnet@gao.gov Automated answering system: (800) 424-5454 or (202) 512-7470
Congressional Relations	Katherine Siggerud, Managing Director, siggerudk@gao.gov, (202) 512-4400, U.S. Government Accountability Office, 441 G Street NW, Room 7125, Washington, DC 20548
Public Affairs	Chuck Young, Managing Director, youngc1@gao.gov, (202) 512-4800 U.S. Government Accountability Office, 441 G Street NW, Room 7149 Washington, DC 20548